YOUR BLOOD
AND ITS CARGO

by Sigmund Kalina

Illustrated by Arabelle Wheatley

SCHOLASTIC BOOK SERVICES
New York Toronto London Auckland Sydney Tokyo

Text copyright © 1974 by Sigmund Kalina. Illustrations copyright © 1974 by Arabelle Wheatley. This edition is published by Scholastic Book Services, a division of Scholastic Magazines, Inc., by arrangement with Lothrop, Lee & Shepard Company, a division of William Morrow & Company, Inc.

12 11 10 9 8 7 6 5 4 3 2   6 7 8 9/7 0 1/8
Printed in the U.S.A.   02

To Susan, my daughter,
for her tender loving care
of her cardiac patients

Each day you awaken to an exciting world around you.

But exciting things are happening inside you all the time.

The Bloodstream

Every second, two million new red blood cells, born in your bones, are swept into your hurrying bloodstream. This life-giving stream, pumped by your heart, races through your body day and night. Its flow never stops.

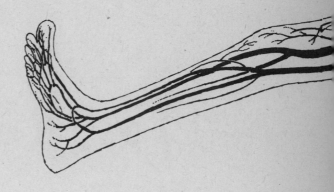

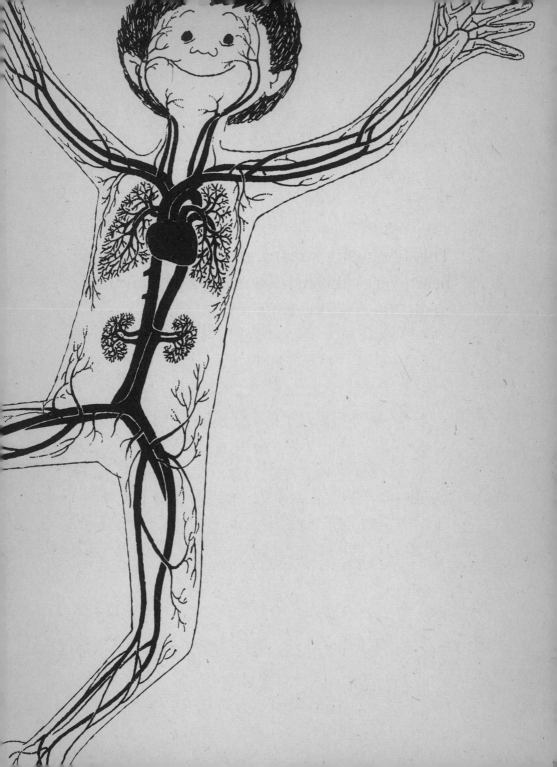

Why do we need blood?

Your body needs food to give you energy — energy to bend, walk, run, or jump, energy to breathe, and more energy to keep your heart pumping over 4,000 gallons of blood each day.

Blood is the remarkable liquid that carries this food and keeps you alive.

How does blood gather food?

On its way through the body, the blood gathers nourishing elements from the food you have digested in your stomach and intestines. It gathers a fresh supply of oxygen from your lungs.

Then the blood delivers its cargo of nutrients and life-supporting oxygen to the billions of living cells throughout your body — brain cells, nerve cells, muscle cells, bone cells, and other kinds of cells.

What is a cell?

Cells are tiny packages of living material which, together, make up any living thing.

Can you see cells?

If you look through a microscope at a thin slice of onion skin, or a splinter of bone, or a muscle fiber inside a chicken leg, you will see that all these different tissues are made up of cells.

Each cell is separated from the other cells by thin walls.

onion skin cells

bone cells

What do cells do?

Each living cell of the body is really a tiny chemical factory. It produces energy by burning up food with the help of oxygen.

This kind of "burning" takes place without a flame.

A burning candle gives off light and heat energy. And the burning up of food inside cells releases energy for all the life activities of the body.

To do its part in these body activities, each living cell needs its own
constant supply of food and oxygen. At
the same time, the wastes produced in
the burning process must be removed.

Your circulating bloodstream delivers
to every living cell in your body the
oxygen and the special food it requires
— such as iron for bone cells — and
collects the wastes and carries them
away.

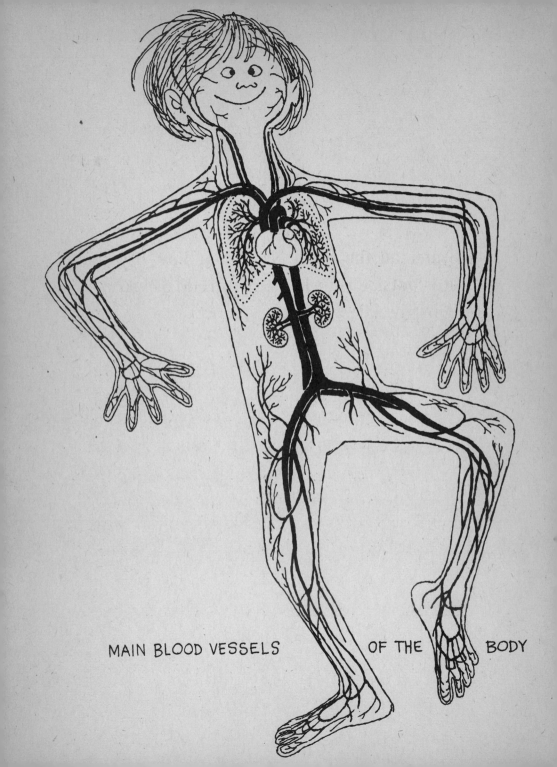

MAIN BLOOD VESSELS OF THE BODY

What makes blood "stream"?

Whenever you are thirsty, you know you need water. But your body requires water all the time. No matter how dry it is outside your body, the inside of you must be kept wet.

In a grown man or woman there are about five to six quarts of blood. About half of this liquid is *plasma*, which is mostly water. This is why blood can stream through your body just as water flows through a pipe.

What carries the bloodstream?

Branching out in all directions, from the top of your head to the tips of your toes, are the tubes that transport your blood and its cargo. Through these vessels the blood travels to all parts of the body.

Some of the vessels are as thick as a jump rope. They are the main arteries and veins. Others are as wide as soda straws. They are smaller arteries and veins. Many are thinner than a hair. They are called capillaries.

All together, the vessels form a network of tubes that reach from deep inside you to just beneath the surface of your skin. If you look at your hands, or the underside of your wrists, you can see dark blue lines. These are tiny tubes filled with blood.

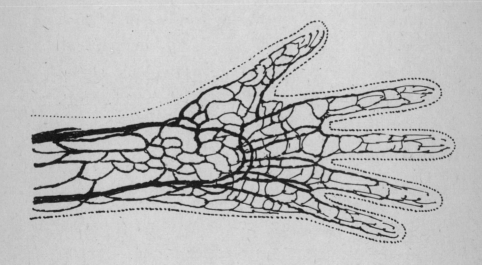

Many people feel faint when they see blood. They think of it as pain. But it is the cut that hurts, not the escaping blood. In fact, a little bleeding helps to cleanse and heal a cut.

What is blood?

If you prick the end of your finger, you will see a drop of blood form. What is this wonder-working liquid? You cannot live without it. What is it made of?

Blood Plasma

The liquid part of your blood, called *plasma*, is a pale yellow, watery liquid that carries dissolved food. (Another part of the blood is a mixture of blood cells, ferried along in the streaming plasma.)

The blood plasma has many important jobs. As the carrier in the body's transport system, it travels through

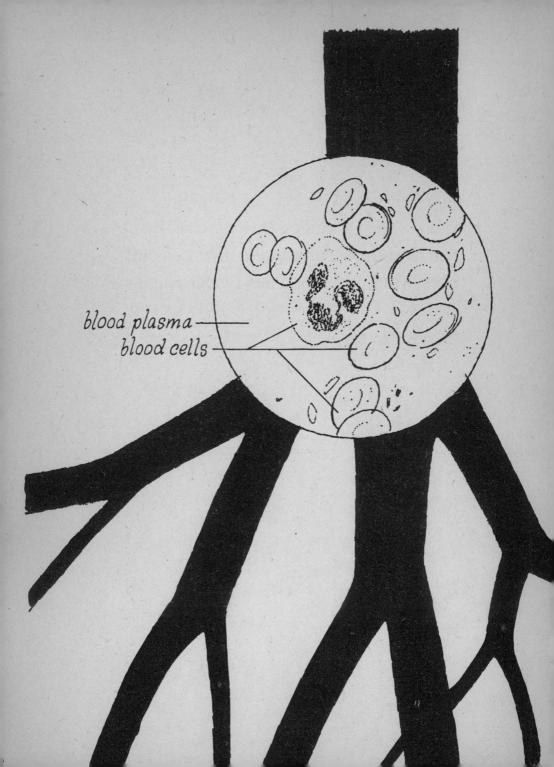

blood plasma
blood cells

branching blood vessels — far out to your fingers and toes, and deep inside your lungs. It passes through the liver, and through soft flesh and spongy bone. Everywhere it goes, the blood plasma brings a mixed cargo of needed chemicals and food elements to the cells.

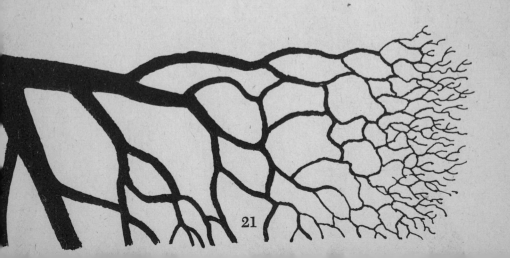

How does food get into plasma?

Feeding the cells of your body is a big, complicated job. The food you eat must be changed before your cells can use it. The parts of your digestive system work like a chemical factory. Your mouth and stomach produce juices —

chemicals and enzymes. Your intestines contain other enzymes and useful bacteria. All of them help to break down the food you have eaten into very tiny particles, called molecules. Just as sugar dissolves in milk, all the foods you eat — peanut butter and jelly, pizza, juicy

hamburgers, ice cream — are digested
into tiny molecules that pass through
the walls of your small intestine into
the blood vessels through *their* walls.
In the blood vessels, the food molecules
are dissolved in the blood plasma, which

swiftly hustles this cargo of food elements to all the living body cells.

How does plasma get rid of body wastes?
The human body is a model of masterful engineering. Not only is the bloodstream continually transporting its cargo of nourishing supplies to the cells; it is also, at the same time, collecting the cells' wastes and transferring them to special organs for removal. If wastes remain too long inside your body, they become harmful and could make you sick. The moving plasma must unload its cargo of unwanted waste molecules without losing all the good, life-giving molecules.

The Kidneys

Some of this work is done in the special organs called kidneys. You have two of them, each shaped like a huge lima bean. The kidneys of a grown-up are about four inches long and three inches wide. Each kidney manufactures urine. The "machinery" that does this is a meshwork of a million tubules, each about one and a quarter inches long. Interlacing blood vessels wind around the kidney tubules. These tubules strain out the harmful wastes from the plasma (which is now moving slowly for this purpose).

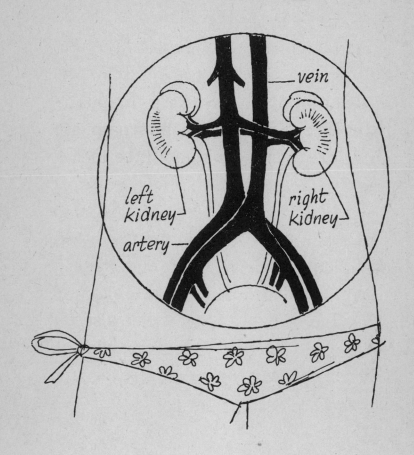

vein

left
kidney

right
kidney

artery

How does this work?

As the plasma passes out through the thin walls of the coiling blood vessels, it seeps into the kidney tubules and deposits its cargo of cell wastes. The liquid waste that collects inside the kidney tubules is called urine.

With much of its wastes left behind, the blood plasma returns to the bloodstream inside the small blood vessels of the kidneys. Still carrying the precious cargo of all the things the body cells need, the bloodstream continues its race through the body.

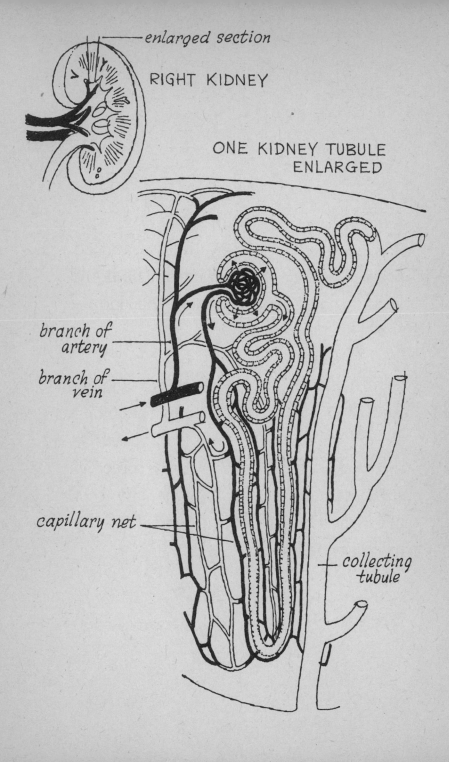

enlarged section

RIGHT KIDNEY

ONE KIDNEY TUBULE
ENLARGED

branch of
artery

branch of
vein

capillary net

collecting
tubule

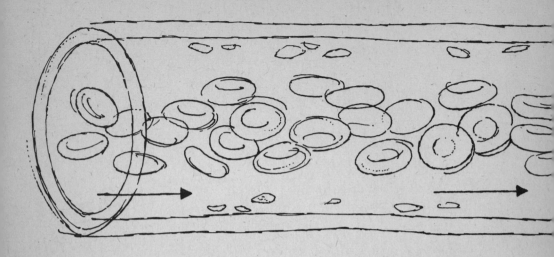

Blood Cells

Blood is more than plasma.

Tumbling, floating, and drifting along in the bloodstream are the blood voyagers. They are much larger than molecules, yet still small enough to travel through the tiniest vessel. They are the blood cells.

These travelers are not just along for the ride; they have important jobs to

perform. The different kinds of blood cells help to guard your health. Without some of them, invading germs would often infect you, make you sick, or even kill you. Without others, you would not be able to stop the bleeding of a cut.

Without still another kind, the body cells would never receive life-giving oxygen, or get rid of the poisonous waste gas which the cells produce as they burn up food.

The oxygen blood cells —
Red Blood Cells

The most numerous of the blood travelers are the red blood cells. They are shaped like little doughnuts with no holes. Millions upon millions are moved along as they crowd the middle of the flowing bloodstream. It would take about three months to count the millions of red cells in one drop of blood the size of a pinhead!

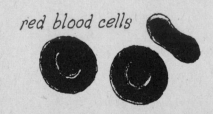

red blood cells

Red blood cells get their color from the hemoglobin molecules they contain. These large hemoglobin molecules are always hungry for oxygen. When you inhale, lots of oxygen molecules are packed into the blood plasma and are quickly drawn to the hemoglobin inside the red blood cells.

Loaded with its cargo of oxygen, each red blood cell is tumbled along in the moving bloodstream. There must always be a steady supply of oxygen to all the cells in the body. Without oxygen, life would be snuffed out, just as a candle flame dies down when its oxygen supply is cut off.

But oxygen (O_2) is not the only cargo carried by the red blood cell. This tiny package of hemoglobin also picks up molecules of carbon dioxide (CO_2), a gas given off by the cells as waste. These molecules are carried to your lungs and then released with the air you breathe out.

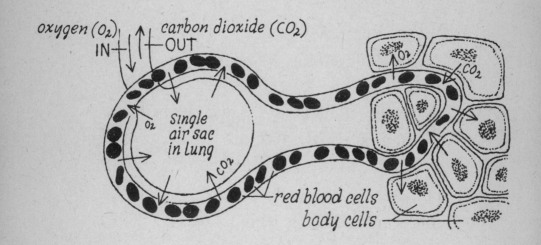

oxygen (O_2) IN — carbon dioxide (CO_2) OUT

O_2 single air sac in lung CO_2

O_2 CO_2

red blood cells
body cells

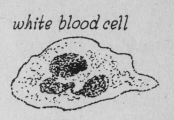

white blood cell

The germ-fighting cells —
White Blood Cells

The emergency squad in the bloodstream is the white blood cells. They move slowly along the sides, away from the mainstream, and are much larger than the red cells and fewer in number. For every white cell found in the blood, there are normally about 600 red cells.

Ever on guard for any foreign invader, these white blood cells police the world inside your body. At times they drift along . . . at other times they move under their own power, and leave the blood through the very thin walls of the hairlike blood vessels.

Outside the blood vessels, the white cells continue their patrol for harmful bacteria that may have entered your body. When they find an enemy, the white cells surround and digest it. In this fashion, the white cells help free the body of disease-producing germs.

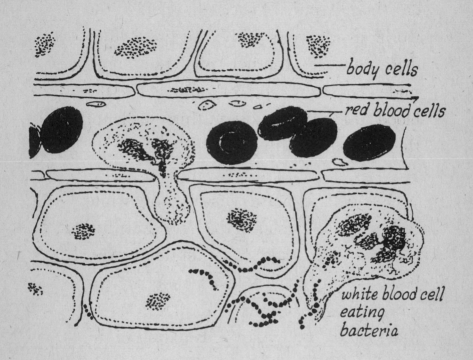

body cells

red blood cells

white blood cell
eating
bacteria

Suppose you have cut your finger!

An alarm is sent out to the wandering white cells in your bloodstream. Germs have swarmed in through the cut in your finger. A battle has begun! If the white cells win, your finger heals.

If the white cells lose, your finger swells, turns red, and feels sore — you have an infection. You know this when you see pus forming . . . dead white cells are piling up! Fortunately, the body keeps on producing more white blood cells.

The blood-clotting cells — the Platelets

The smallest of the blood passengers are the platelets. Oval in shape, and about one-third the size of the red blood cells, these cells slide along in the streaming blood plasma, always ready to plug any sudden leak.

To stop the bleeding of a cut, both the plasma and the platelets work together. Let us see how this happens:

Platelets are not very strong; they fall apart very easily. As they cruise along in the bloodstream, they are protected by the soft, smooth walls of the blood vessels.

If, for some reason, platelets bump against a rough spot, such as cells that are injured from cuts or bruises, they explode and begin to stick to the ruptured place, forming a plug in the hole.

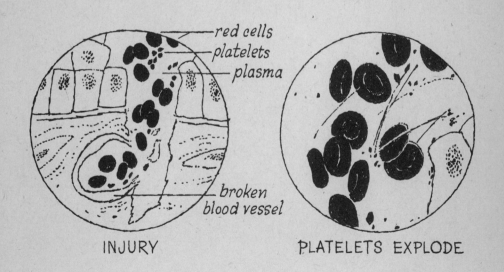

INJURY   PLATELETS EXPLODE

At the same time, escaping molecules from the platelets flash messages
through the plasma to hidden molecules,
which, like magic, shape into soft, long,
sticky threads drifting in the blood
plasma.

These blood fibers lace the platelet
plug in place, trapping red blood cells

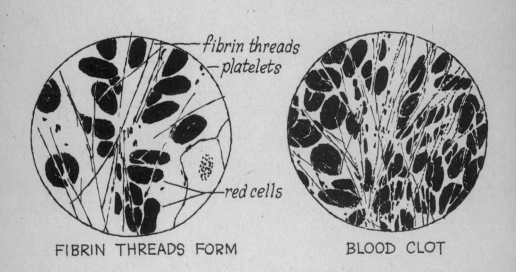

FIBRIN THREADS FORM   BLOOD CLOT

in a jellylike web. A blood clot now seals the opening.

Where do blood cells come from?

Although the billions of blood cells spend their lives in the circulating blood, they are born outside the mainstream. Most of these cells are produced in your bones.

Inside the hard outer layer of bone is a soft spongy material called marrow, of which there are two kinds. Red marrow contains large amounts of blood. Yellow marrow serves as a storage place for fat.

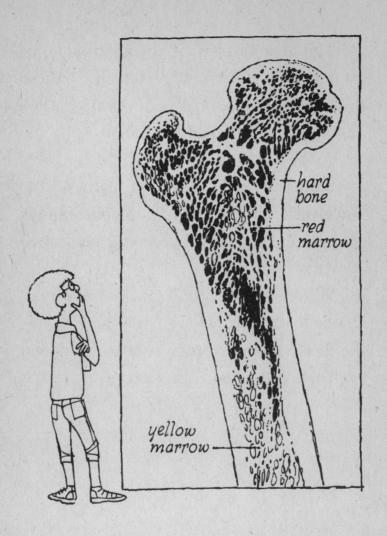

hard
bone

red
marrow

yellow
marrow

The red marrow is the birthplace of the body's red blood cells. Once these young cells are fully developed, they escape into the bloodstream.

Bone is richly supplied with a fine lacework of branching blood vessels bringing food and oxygen and transporting wastes.

You remember that two million red blood cells are born each second. Two million also disintegrate. A red blood cell lives for about 120 days.

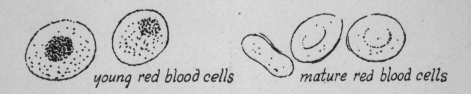

young red blood cells   mature red blood cells

What controls the direction of blood?

Blood does not flow aimlessly from one vessel to another. The body has its own built-in directional system by which the blood moves.

Blood is pumped by the heart to the lungs, where it picks up oxygen. Then the bright, oxygen-rich blood returns to the heart, which pumps it through the aorta to the other arteries. Arteries are blood vessels with strong elastic walls. They expand at each powerful spurt of the oxygen-fresh blood as it shoots through the vessels with each heartbeat. The main artery is the aorta. It is about one inch wide, with walls as much as one-eighth of an inch thick.

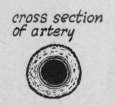

cross section of artery

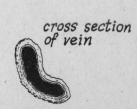

cross section of vein

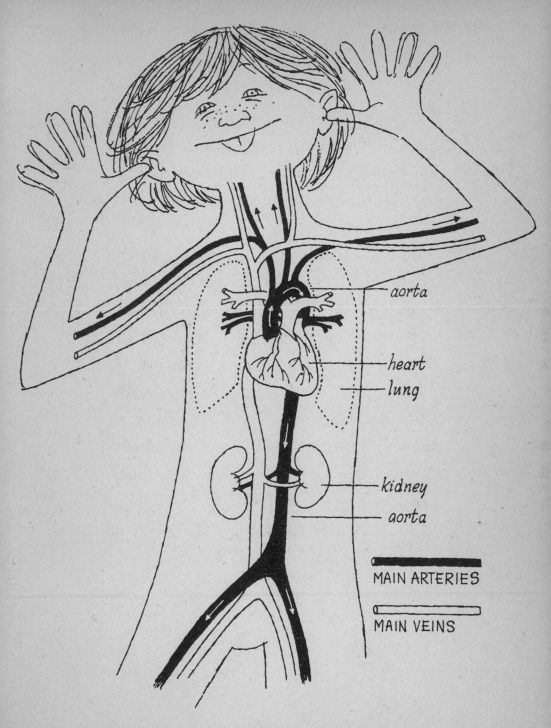

aorta

heart

lung

kidney

aorta

MAIN ARTERIES

MAIN VEINS

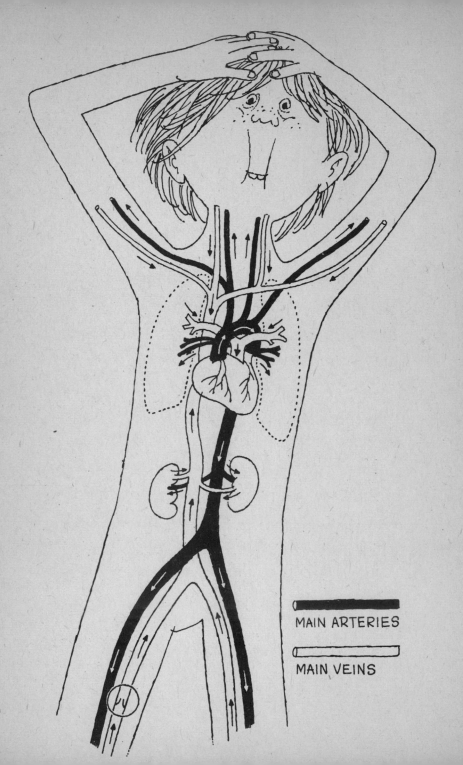

MAIN ARTERIES

MAIN VEINS

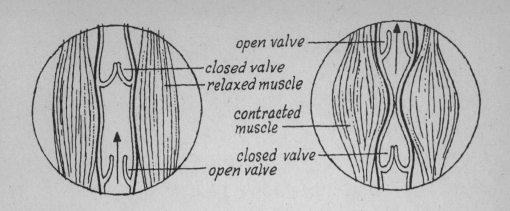

open valve
closed valve
relaxed muscle
contracted muscle
closed valve
open valve

After circulating all through the body, the dark, carbon dioxide-filled blood returns to the heart and lungs through the veins. It is now under much less pressure. The blood flowing down from the head is helped along by the pull of gravity. The blood coming back to the heart from the lower parts of your body is pushed upward through the veins by the squeezing muscles surrounding them.

Tiny, fleshy, hingelike flaps, called valves, keep the blood from flowing backward in the veins.

Hundreds of years ago, scientists did not know how the blood reached the toes and returned to the heart. It was thought that the blood flowed back and forth in the same blood vessels, just as the tides flow onto the beach and back again into the sea.

Then, in the early sixteen hundreds, an English doctor named William Harvey discovered the truth about blood

WILLIAM HARVEY

vessels. He learned, after many experiments, that the blood travels from the heart, circulates through the body, and then returns. He found that the blood in any blood vessel flows in only one direction.

But how was it possible for the blood to flow from the arteries into the veins on its way back to the heart? William Harvey reasoned that there must be some connection between the arteries and the veins, but he could not find the joining vessels.

Capillaries

A short time after Harvey's death, an Italian scientist named Marcello Malpighi made a great discovery. While examining a frog's lung through a microscope, he saw the networks of capillaries. These are the tiniest of all blood vessels.

Nutrients and oxygen pass through the walls of the capillaries to the cells. The capillaries also enable the blood to pass between the smallest arteries and the smallest veins.

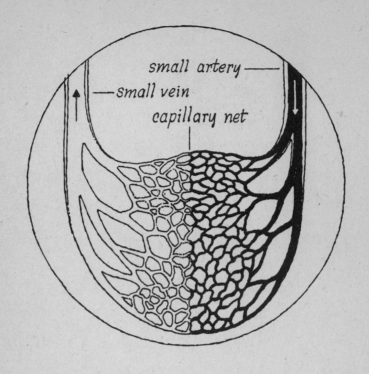

small artery
small vein
capillary net

Although the arteries, veins, and capillaries follow branching routes, they are all connected. Together, they form a web of winding vessels.

Blood never leaks from these vessels

— unless one is cut, or it bursts at a weak place in its wall.

If you could take all your blood vessels and place them end to end, they would reach two-and-one-half times around the equator — about sixty thousand miles!

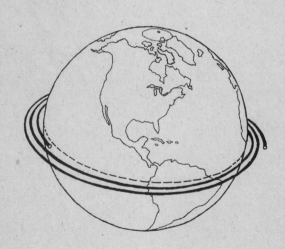

What about the heart?

Inside your chest — just behind your breastbone, between your lungs, and leaning to one side — is the central pump. It drives the blood through the thousands of miles of pipeline, keeping flesh and bone alive and healthy.

This living pump, the heart, is no larger than a man's fist, and weighs about eleven ounces. It is a masterpiece of design.

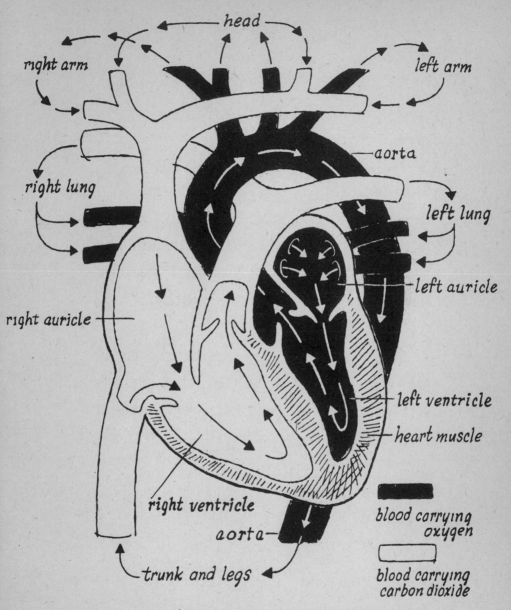

FLOW OF BLOOD THROUGH THE HEART

The heart is a powerful organ with walls made of tough muscle. It never stops working as long as you live.

Each day, the heart pumps about seventeen *tons* of blood. Yet, for the blood to make its tour through the body and back again to the heart takes less than a minute!

Feel your heart beating. The lower left chamber of your heart, the left ventricle, is rhythmically contracting, squeezing blood into the aorta. (See diagram on previous page.) This is what you hear as a heartbeat.

How fast does your heart beat?

At birth, your heart beats about 140 times a minute. Now, your heart probably beats about 90 times a minute. When you are grown, it will beat about 70 to 80 times a minute. Of course, your heart beats faster when you are excited or exercising.

How fast do other hearts beat?

It is known that the heart of each kind of animal has a rhythmic beat and a pace all its own. It takes as long for a frog's heart to beat 25 times as for a canary's heart to beat 800 times!

Here are some *approximate* heartbeat measurements that scientists have recorded for various kinds of animals. Many things, such as age, size, or temperature, affect the heartbeat rate.

HEART OF	BEATS PER MINUTE *about:*
Bat (mammal)	740
Hummingbird	650
Mouse (mammal)	580
Robin (bird)	565
Duck (bird)	270
Rabbit (mammal)	200
Dolphin (mammal)	150
Spider (arachnid)	130
Cat or Dog (mammal)	120
Ostrich (bird)	65
Horse (mammal)	44
Lion (mammal)	40
Trout (fish)	38
Crocodile (reptile)	35
Shark ((fish)	26
Whale (mammal)	16
Turtle (reptile)	7

Minute by minute, second by second, your bloodstream circulates with its precious cargo through sixty thousand miles of tubes. Every second, as long as your heart beats, your blood and its cargo will continue to nourish your living, growing body.

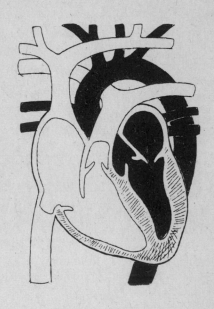

Index

fibrin, 42
frog, 52, 60

germs, 31, 36, 39
gravity, 49

Harvey, William, 50; picture of
    51
heal, 18, 39
heart, 6, 8, 46, 47, 49, 56; dia-
    gram of 57; 58, 59, 60
heartbeat, 46, 58; rate of 59,
    60, 61
hemoglobin, 33

infection, 31, 39
intestines, 8, 23; small intes-
    tine 24
iron, 13

kidneys, 26; diagram of 27; 28,
    29, 47

liver, 21
lungs, 8, 21; diagram of lung
    air sac 34; 46, 47, 49, 56, 57

Malpighi, Marcello, 52

microscope, 10, 11, 52
molecules, 23, 24, 25, 43
mouth, 22
muscle cells, 9

nerve cells, 9
nutrients, 9, 53

oxygen, 8, 9, 12, 13, 32, 33, 34,
    45, 53, 57

plasma, 15, 25, 28, 40, 42
platelets, 40; diagram of 41;
    42
pus, 39

stomach, 8, 22

tissues, 11
tubules, of kidneys, 26, 28, 29

urine, 26, 28

valves, of veins, 49
ventricle, 57, 58

wastes, 13, 25, 32, 45
water, 15